# Gram Can

"a devotional
and journal
for grandmothers"

written by
## Emmie R Werner

illustrated by
## Jack Foster

**Halo**
PUBLISHING
INTERNATIONAL

Halo Publishing International
7550 WIH-10 #800, PMB 2069,
San Antonio, TX 78229

First Edition, October 2023
ISBN: 978-1-63765-501-6
Library of Congress Control Number: 2023917613

Halo Publishing International is a self-publishing company that publishes adult fiction and non-fiction, children's literature, self-help, spiritual, and faith-based books. We continually strive to help authors reach their publishing goals and provide many different services that help them do so. We do not publish books that are deemed to be politically, religiously, or socially disrespectful, or books that are sexually provocative, including erotica. Halo reserves the right to refuse publication of any manuscript if it is deemed not to be in line with our principles. Do you have a book idea you would like us to consider publishing? Please visit www.halopublishing.com for more information.

*GRAM CAN* is dedicated to Grandma Willhelm, who lived in a different time. While wearing her apron, she gathered vegetables and fruit, dried our tears, and held us on her lap.

But, most of all, I want to dedicate *GRAM CAN* to the grandma who feels life has passed her by, who feels she is not important, who feels she has reached the end. Let me encourage you with God's word: "They will still bear fruit in old age, they will stay fresh and green" (Psalm 92:14, New International Version). "Your latter days will be very great" (Job 8:7, English Standard Version). This is my prayer for Grams.

# Day 1

"I am able to do all things through the one who strengthens me" (Philippians 4:13, New English Translation).

Through the one who strengthens me...I am not saying we are old...but...I find myself relying more and more on the Lord to be able to do things. BUT, it just might be I'm finally figuring out what I should have known all my life. I can only do what I do because of Him, who gives me strength.

## Journal

CAN you recall a time when you relied on the Lord for strength?

## Remember:

I am able to do all things through the ONE who strengthens me.

# Day 2

"And my God will fully satisfy every need of yours according to His riches in glory in Christ Jesus" (Philippians 4:19, New Revised Standard Version, Anglicized).

Three words caught my attention when I read this translation–*fully, satisfy,* and *need.* I thought, *Fully satisfy? Isn't that just like our God. He didn't just say He will take care of us, but He will fully satisfy us.* To me, that comes with a hard-to-describe feeling of contentment, completeness, and a knowing in my innermost being that would come the closest to being described as fully satisfied. When I look at my life, I can say He certainly has, overwhelmingly above what I could have imagined, fully satisfied all my *needs.*

## Journal

CAN you describe that fully satisfied feeling from God in your life?

## Remember:

God will fully satisfy every need of yours.

# Day 3

"Be strong because God has given us His Spirit. And His Spirit does not cause us to be afraid. Instead, His Spirit causes us to be powerful to serve God. He helps us to love God and other people. And He helps us to control ourselves properly" (2 Timothy 1:7, EasyEnglish Version).

"For God has not given us a spirit of fear, but of power and of love and a sound mind" (2 Timothy 1:7, New King James Version).

This Scripture is so encouraging. Be strong in Him. Know no fear in Him. Love others in Him. Have a sound mind in Him (especially at this stage in life!). And then I read "and rule ourselves properly in Him," and it made me stop. What does that mean to me–rule myself properly? How?

Make sure I keep God at the center of my life. Read His word. Pray. Honor what honors Him. Care for myself, knowing my body is a temple of the Holy Spirit.

So do I hit all the marks? No, but I know God is with me–He will help me *rule myself properly.*

## Journal

CAN you think of an area of your life in which you need/want God to help you rule yourself properly?

## Remember:

Be strong because God has given us His Spirit.

## Day 4

"God has been kind to me so that I can serve Him. Because of that, I can say this to every one of you: Do not think that you are better than you really are. Instead, think about yourself carefully. Decide how much God has helped you to trust Him. Then you will know how to serve Him well" (Romans 12:3, EasyEnglish Version).

As I reflect on this passage, I can't help but reflect on my life. God has been so kind to my family and me, over the years, in His care, guidance, and showing us the way. He has shown us He is a trustworthy God. Trusting our kids, and now grandkids, to Him shows me areas in my life where my faith is weak. But I see that, where I am weak, He is strong. How can I not want to serve Him? Not because He expects it, but because I love Him!

## Journal

CAN you list the times God has shown your family and you kindness, grace, and mercy?

## Remember:

God has been kind to me. Decide how much God has helped you to trust Him.

# Day 5

"Lord, you are my Light and my Savior, so why should I be afraid of anyone? The Lord is where my life is safe, so I will be afraid of no one" (Psalm 27:1, Easy-to-Read Version).

When I read this translation of Psalm 27, two things stand out. He is my Savior, and because He is my Savior, my life is safe. What a comforting promise! Even when everything around me feels unsure and shaky, He keeps me and those around me safe. When I think about my prayers, many of them are in thanksgiving for keeping all of us safe, including our kids and grandkids—IT IS HIS PROMISE; we are safe in Him. Thank you, Jesus!

## Journal

CAN you recall the times you knew Jesus had kept you safe?

## Remember:

The Lord is where my life is safe.

# Day 6

"My little children, you belong to God. You have won against those people with a false message. You have been able to do that because God's Holy Spirit is in you. He is more powerful than the spirit that belongs to this world" (1 John 4:4, EasyEnglish Version).

My little children. When was the last time you thought of yourself as a little child? ☺ But when God looks at you, that is what He sees—His child. You have stood against the snares of the devil, been faithful to Him, stormed the heavens for your family, church family, and friends. You have stood strong for Him your whole life. And still He looks at you as His child to be loved and cared for. The God of the universe considers me His child; it is almost more than I can comprehend, but I BELIEVE.

## Journal

CAN you make a list of your life's wins?

## Remember:

My little children, you belong to God.

# Day 7

"But I thank God! He has won against sin because of what Christ has done. Christ is our leader, and we show that He is the winner. We also help people to know about Christ. That knowledge is like a lovely smell that comes to people everywhere" (2 Corinthians 2:14, EasyEnglish Version).

Imagine your life in Christ as a lovely smell. Whomever you are with, whatever you are doing, He is leading and guiding you to share Christ. I am thankful our job is to show His love. He will do the rest. We do not have to perform to get His praise; our job is to share His love and His fragrance with all those He puts in our path. Especially our *grands*. ☺

## Journal

CAN you make a list of everyone with whom you will share Jesus with over the next few days?

## Remember:

We also help people to know about Christ.

# Day 8

"For it is not from man that we draw our life, but from God as we are being joined to Jesus, the Anointed One. And now He is our God-given wisdom, our virtue, our holiness, and our redemption" (1 Corinthians 1:30, The Passion Translation).

We draw our life from God, and He IS our life! Looking back through our lives, it is easy to see where God has been our redemption, where He has been our virtue and our wisdom. How does He want us to use this wisdom? Pass it along. For us, He has given us a harvest field–our grandkids! ☺ Before them, we need to live our lives full of God's wisdom, virtue, and holiness. Live the complete life Jesus has for you today.

## Journal

CAN you list the ways/times you have seen God's wisdom in your life today, yesterday, or last week?

## Remember:

For it is not from man that we draw our life, but from God as we are being joined in Jesus.

## Day 9

"Then I remember something that fills me with hope. The Lord's kindness never fails! If he had not been merciful, we would have been destroyed. The Lord can always be trusted to show mercy each morning" (Lamentations 3:21–23, Contemporary English Version).

For those of us who have had many "new mornings," this Scripture is so full of encouragement. Looking back on our lives, we can see how God protected and led us when we didn't know what to do. Usually we didn't understand what He was doing until we were on the other side. Share with your family, especially your grands, what God has done for you.

## Journal

CAN you make a list of the times God has been merciful to you?

## Remember:

The Lord can always be trusted to show mercy each morning.

# Day 10

"Casting all your cares [all your anxieties, all your worries, and all your concerns, once and for all] on Him, for He cares about you [with deepest affection and watches over you very carefully]" (1 Peter 5:7, Amplified Bible).

When you read this Scripture, you have to get God's point of view. What He says, He means! ALL our concerns, worries, and anxieties are His. Even though our kids are grown and have kids of their own, we must trust God to watch over them. We need to turn over to Him all our hopes and dreams for our kids and our grandkids, for He loves them with deepest affection–and you too!

## Journal

CAN you give Him your concerns and worries? Put them in the can?

## Remember:

He cares about you with deepest affection!

# Day 11

"At last we have freedom, for Christ has set us free! We must always cherish this truth and firmly refuse to go back into the bondage of our past" (Galatians 5:1, The Passion Translation).

Hindsight is 20/20. We can dwell on our failures and mistakes, or we can cherish our freedom in Christ. Which is of more benefit to our family and friends? We should live in such a state of freedom from our past that others would wonder and ask, "What is it about you?"

"Well, let me tell you about my Jesus and how He set me free."

## Journal

CAN you write your testimony and be ready to share?

## Remember:

At last we have freedom, for Christ has set us free.

# Day 12

"So now the case is closed. There remains no accusing voice of condemnation against those who are joined in life-union with Jesus, the Anointed One" (Romans 8:1, The Passion Translation).

The term *life-union* struck a sweet chord in my spirit. To have lived a life-union with Jesus, what a blessing! To be able to say I have served Him my whole life and continue to do so. The life-union with Jesus begins the moment we ask Him into our hearts. For some, it happened when we were very small; for others, when they were middle-aged; and, maybe, for still others... yesterday or even today. When Jesus sees you *today*, no matter when you said yes to Him, He sees a life-union. Oh, so thankful!

## Journal

CAN you tell your grands about the time you asked Jesus into your heart?

## Remember:

There remains no accusing voice of condemnation against those who are joined in life-union with Jesus.

# Day 13

"Teaching them to observe everything that I have commanded you; and, lo, I am with you always [remaining with you perpetually–regardless of circumstance, and on every occasion], even to the end of the age" (Matthew 28:20, Amplified Bible).

Has someone ever asked you a question to which you gave a greatly detailed answer? It seems to me that is what Jesus is doing in this Scripture. He is saying He is always with us; He never leaves us, no matter our circumstances or our attitude; and He never leaves our side. It makes me pause and wonder what I have done, thought, or said that made His heart grieve (even unintentionally). Yet He did not leave me. Oh, thank you, Jesus, you are with me to the end of my age.

## Journal

CAN you tell your grands about the times Jesus was closer than a friend to you?

## Remember:

I am with you always.

# Day 14

"Christ redeemed us from that self-defeating, cursed life by absorbing it completely into Himself...He became a curse, and at the same time dissolved the curse...We are *all* able to receive God's life, His Spirit, in and with us, by believing..." (Galatians 3:13-14, The Message).

*Absorbing it completely into Himself*—think about that. Before you and I were born, Jesus bore all our sins on the cross. All the times we were discouraged, depressed, felt we had been wronged—Jesus already took care of that on the cross. We have freedom; you and I are free! And what do we need to do to have that freedom? Simple. BELIEVE!

## Journal

CAN you make a list of things in which you believe?

## Remember:

We are ALL able to receive God's life, His Spirit, in and with us by believing.

# Day 15

"Not that I speak from [any personal] need, for I have learned to be content [and self-sufficient through Christ, satisfied to the point where I am not disturbed or uneasy] regardless of my circumstances" (Philippians 4:11, Amplified Bible).

To the point that I am not disturbed or uneasy, when I read this, I picture myself in a hammock, on a porch, feeling the breeze, and reading a good book. That feeling of peace in Jesus that really can't be explained—only felt. Our job is to be in His peace, no matter what our circumstances. To do this, we need to be in His word, be with Him, and fellowship with His people. So be at peace, content, and satisfied, regardless of your circumstances, because Christ is in you. (And enjoy your hammock. ☺)

# Journal

CAN you describe your place of peace?

## Remember:

I have learned to be content...regardless of my circumstances.

# Day 16

"God had Christ, who was sinless, take our sin so that we might receive God's approval through Him" (2 Corinthians 5:21, GOD'S WORD Translation).

We all seek approval, no matter how old we are. Approval from our parents, siblings, friends, teachers, coworkers, AND grands! It doesn't matter what age we are; we all want people to like us. God liked us so much that He put the burden of our sins on His Son so that we could be accepted and loved by God. Our job is to accept the fact that Jesus did this for us. By asking Jesus into our heart, we gain God's stamp of approval—what a deal!

## Journal

How CAN you show God's approval to your grands?

## Remember:

We receive God's approval through Him (Jesus).

# Day 17

"So, because of all the things that God does for us, we can say this: If God is working on our behalf, nobody can really do anything against us" (Romans 8:31, EasyEnglish Version).

It would have been amazing to have kept a list of all the things God has done for me in my lifetime. Every day, He takes care of me—finding a parking space, traveling safely, receiving a phone call or text just when I needed it, healing me, giving me a job when I didn't even know I needed one at the time, and many, many more things.

You know it's never too late to make a list. Let's start today. "Thank you, Jesus, for being my Savior" is at the top of my list.

## Journal

CAN you list everything God has done for you today?
Share the list with your grands.

## Remember:

So, because of all the things that God does for us, we
can say this: If God is working on our behalf, nobody
can really do anything against us.

# Day 18

"But God has given us His Spirit. This is why we don't think the same way that the people of this world think. This is also why we can recognize the blessing God has given us" (1 Corinthians 2:12, Contemporary English Version).

When I read this translation of first book of Corinthians, it was like a seal of approval from the Lord. We don't think the way the rest of the world does because of the Holy Spirit. We recognize His blessings in our normal, everyday lives because of the Holy Spirit. Let's stop today and thank God for sending His Holy Spirit to be with us, guide us, teach us, and show us how much God loves us...every day!

## Journal

CAN you make a list of the ways the Holy Spirit worked in your life today?

## Remember:

This is also why we can recognize the blessings God has given us.

# Day 19

"No, in all these things we have complete victory through Him who loved us" (Romans 8:37, New English Translation).

"Because God loves us, none of these troubles can ever beat us. He makes us win against them" (Romans 8:37, EasyEnglish Version).

So today I couldn't decide which translation said what I wanted to say. At this stage of my life, I can see that God has brought me through troubles to victories. How can we show our loved ones, especially our grands, how much God loves them? Easy! Tell them your story...and love them!

## Journal

CAN you share your story with one of your grands today?

## Remember:

We have complete victory through Him who loves us!

# Day 20

"And if anyone longs to be wise, ask God for wisdom, and He will give it! He won't see your lack of wisdom as an opportunity to scold you over your failures, but He will overwhelm your failures with His generous grace" (James 1:5, The Passion Translation).

When we reach a certain point in our lives, we are able to look back and realize that what we saw as failures God used as opportunities to help us gain wisdom. What are we going to do with that wisdom? I believe that is why God gave us grands. At some point in our lives, our kids come to believe that we are wise, but our grands, from the very start, accept us as always being their greatest champions. Hmmm...just like Jesus...OUR greatest champion.

## Journal

CAN you spend time with your grands today, imparting some of your God-given wisdom?

## Remember:

If anyone longs to be wise, ask God for wisdom, and He will give it.

# Day 21

"I have told you these things, so that in Me you may have [perfect] peace. In the world you have tribulation and distress and suffering, but be courageous [be confident, be undaunted, be filled with joy]; I have overcome the world [My conquest is accomplished, My victory abiding.]" (John 16:33, Amplified Bible).

I am not sure how to end this twenty-one-day journey for Grams. As Grams, we have lived through tribulations, suffering, and distress. God wants us to pass on to our grands that because of Jesus, we are victorious. We are filled with His joy. So we finish this journey with confidence in accomplishing all He has planned for us. We have been given great treasures in our grandchildren. Be a "grand" Gram.

## Journal

CAN you make a list of what you believe God wants you to do with and for your grands?

## Remember:

Be courageous; be filled with joy. I have overcome the world.

# Gram "Cans"

### Day 1

Teach your grand to CAN.

### Day 2

Make CAN-dy with your grand, and enjoy it!

### Day 3

Take a walk along a CAN-al with your grand.

### Day 4

Go CAN-oeing with your grand.

### Day 5

Have a CAN-did conversation with your grand.

### Day 6

Plant CAN-na lily bulbs with your grand.

### Day 7

Go to a CAN-dle store with your grand.

### Day 8

Paint a CAN-vas with your grand.

### Day 9

Sit under a CAN-opy with your grand.

### Day 10

Bake a cake using CAN-ola oil with your grand.

### Day 11

Take a walk with a CAN-ine and your grand.

### Day 12

Plan (or dream about) a trip to CAN-cun with your grand.

## Day 13

Go to a CAN-tata with your grand.

## Day 14

Eat CAN-taloupe with your grand.

## Day 15

CAN-cel everything, and spend the day with your grand.

## Day 16

Go to a pet store and watch the CAN-aries with your grand.

## Day 17

Explore the Grand CAN-yon virtually with your grand.

## Day 18

Fill a CAN-teen, and go for a walk with your grand.

## Day 19

Do the CAN-CAN with your grand.

## Day 20

Grands' day to choose what you CAN do.

## Day 21

Grams' day to choose what you CAN do.

These twenty-one Gram CANs are just suggestions. Any time you spend with your grands is a blessed time. In fact, God tells us that is what we are supposed to do: "Now that I am old and my hair is gray, don't leave me, God. I must tell the next generation about your power and greatness" (Psalm 71:18, Easy-to-Read Version). You thought of everything, God. I am so thankful.

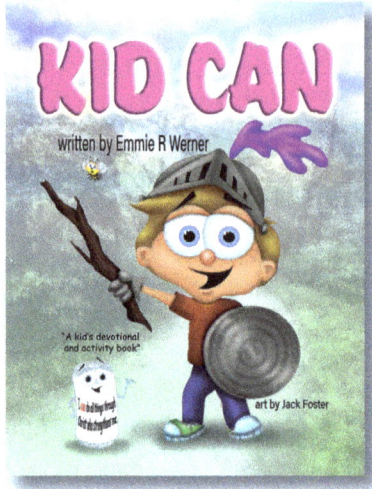

## Kid Can

ISBN Hardcover: 978-1-63765-515-3
ISBN Paperback: 978-1-63765-046-2

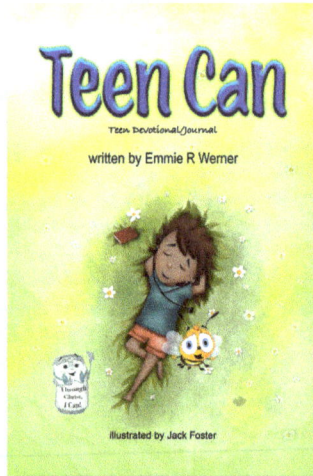

## Teen Can

ISBN Hardcover: 978-1-63765-516-0
ISBN Paperback: 978-1-63765-186-5

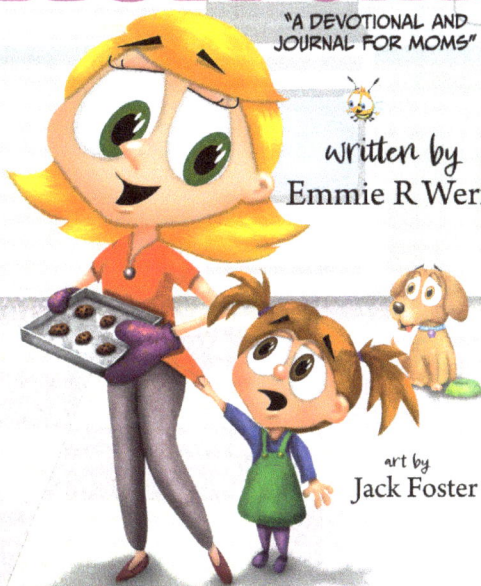

# Mom Can

ISBN Hardcover: 978-1-63765-375-3
ISBN Paperback: 978-1-63765-374-6

www.ingramcontent.com/pod-product-compliance
Lightning Source LLC
LaVergne TN
LVHW070012090426
835509LV00041B/3475